The Long Net

Poems about the great game of basketball

BOOKS BY IRV BROUGHTON

ESPN: The Untold Story (and Stuart Evey)
Forever Remembered: The Fliers of WWII
Hangar Talk: Conversations with American Fliers
A Good Man: Fathers and Sons in Poetry and Prose
The Writer's Mind, Vol. III
The Writer's Mind, Vol. II
The Writer's Mind, Vol. I
Producers on Producing
Reindeers Don't Eat Trees: Anti-Drug Poems
The Art of the Interview in Television, Radio and Film
The Blessing of the Fleet: Poems

The Long Net

Poems about the great game of basketball.

Irv Broughton

Open Look Books

Spokane, Washington

ACKNOWLEDGEMENTS

"Rainbow over Florida" appeared in *Crosscurrents.*
"Shooter's Roll" appeared in *The Wire Harp.*
"The Old Place Back" appeared in *The Iconoclast.*

Thanks to Mike and Linda Chase, Connie Broughton, Christopher Howell, Bob Zeller, Betsy Ward, and James J. McAuley. Special thanks to Dennis Held for his assistance and support.

Cover art "Rebound" & cover design by Josh Frost.
Author's photograph by Nicole Solum.
Book design by Karen Checkoway.

Printed in America.

Open Look Books
P.O. Box 8316
Spokane, Washington 99203

irvbroughton.com

ISBN 978-0-912350-06-6

CONTENTS

For McKenzie, Sayer, and Callie
— and Hoopsters everywhere

"Watch 'em chuck it from the seats."
— Shooter, from *Hoosiers*

"The crowd leaves with the winner...
all calling their long loyalty..."
— Dante Alighieri

"Above the indistinguishable roar of many feet,
I feel the presence of the sun, of the immense
forces of the universe, and beyond these,
the sense of the eternal now..."
— Richard Jefferies

THE STRANDS OF VICTORY

I've cut down the net
One small twist and
Freed it from
The impulse-traffic of balls
Firing through

And kept it in my topmost
Drawer, almost child-
Proof like a lover's braid
For I must have
Admired it, and when
We moved I carried
It in myself

And surrendered
Again and again
To victory.

HOOPS, FOREVER

I.
The gym's replaced by a facility
Clean as a napkin; the Boone Street
Barn they called it, and voters
Flocked to modernize, bring

In high-class acts. The biggest swans
Prevailed and finally when the barn fell
Beside itself, I felt a dark cloud shift.

II.
Some Native Americans lay stones around
Their tents and the shapes still build
A solid divide after all these years.
I decide to remain outside, ignore Metallica

Peeking through the crowd, ready to pour
Groupies out like sparkling water. I sidestep
To the wood stove in the Burke, Idaho
Gymnasium, waltz like a dancer on one

Leg in the elevated court of Sanford High —
The night where Cayll got forty and I fed
Him all night and no one toppled off.
I feel my ideal court roll when players thunder

Down the uneven length, move like piano
Legs, and the keys somehow clatter out
A few notes, chasing the point guard
With a message I might hear. The musician

Has stopped playing, and the audience catches
In silence. Everything is over — and I must drive on.

CHUCK TAYLOR'S SHOES

For Roger Waller

We studied our gym shoes hard
When Chuck Taylor himself showed up
To practice: his name sat ankle-high,
Weak canvas to guide against sprains

With a star inside a rubber circle
On Converse All-Star high-tops.
A small vein passing through a heart.
Chuck, we'd been told, had played pro

But God alone knew when or where.
The score seemed a dark continent
Away as he stood near half court.
Nestled on a wing he flicked it underhand

And we watched the ball climb like a homer,
Headed for the unlikely basket
And watched it settling in with a slosh
Like rain-splash off leaves.

His shoes, firm on the Converse ground,
Turned him to target beyond the green line,
Sent the ball to basket and with more
Makes, and I miss, each shot I take
In my old, new All-Stars becomes
A graceful bow from Chuck's return.

LIVING HIGH

For Terry Swanger

When asked about the altitude of a game location, Coach Tarkanian said it shouldn't matter: the game is played indoors.

Some places the snap of baskets
Kicks up none of the red dust of
Albuquerque, standing more than
A mile high. The Sandia Mountains

Hold back the high-flying sky,
Beckoning unto the Running
Rebs to enter the call of the passing
Lanes, take the honest time, look inside

The net, see it blink there as if
It too breathes. But the Pit deepens wider
And as game approaches, the sky resists
And the players begin to

Struggle in the flimsy heat deemed
Mountain air, unable to rise from terre
Firma, this element we must climb.
With the first skyward dunk, no one will

Wave off the landing, and like someone
Who has broken with the earth, the team
Flies again and again. You were right: no air,
Except the low ceiling of a deflated ball, will

Slow you now. And it should be clear
As the contest speeds along
The doors will creak open and
Excitement climb beyond the grade of fever

Pitch, and summoning like coach will blow
The roof off the stubborn Pit, and all of that little
Worry, be duped by the soft-breeze
Victory come like light-bearing players.

LEATHER BASKETBALLS

What once sailed, floated, led
The way to victory, a circle
Of backspin, a surge of zephyrs
Now rests like caged animals
Where they sink, settle in
As if they must try to find

The most perfect position to dream.
One ball's gathered like
A snub-nosed pig; another
Lop-sided, the contested stool
A heavy-set coach in his dotage
Sat in to whimper instruction.

I move closer, feel the streamers
Of net fall over team shoulders
And we take to our narrow caves
Of sight like ancient history.
Anything of the flesh that lasts,
Like cattle heading somewhere west.
In the janitor's hardened hands,

The real leather balls rise
As if they know where they have been,
Will not shed their resilient skins,
Fraying deep, the black
Bladder showing through, a slight
Leak and sigh that signifies.

THE OLD PLACE BACK

With my basketball
As a small child, I slept,
Held it like a soft breast.

Now much older, I lie
On my side, cup
My head with an open

Hand, as if to contain
The fount of hoop
Dreams in sleep. As I age

Beyond the play lots,
The silver gyms and lattice
Lines longer than shadow

Of a player, any player,
I carry the only shot
We get.

RAINBOW SHOT ACROSS FLORIDA

For Steven Wood Igou

Just three times
The ball was ahead
Of me, flying
Like destiny
Of a Key
Largo night toward
A hoop sinking
Under rain. I could scarcely
See myself as I watched
The table of landscape —
My feet set themselves,
The feel of grass soft
As sleep. Even the petals
Of rain could not
Contain you in its
Particoloured arc.
I could have played
In this surrendered
Light for hours, making
The shot go down
The same way: the ball
Awash on the lee
Side of water, like a horse
Escaping the shadow
Of its tail, the entered
Luminescence, the gauge
Of sky tested time
After time and found solid.

ON BUYING A HOOP

For Sayer

This should be as simple
As falling across the room

At Christmas to find one
Orange circle, without the leg

Of post that had returned
To a slump beneath the tree.

But this is not the same:
The ready-made pole and back-

Board shows the particle
Board still sticking to itself

Like self-hatred, the hoop's
Net tied off in a quick

Vasectomy, two balls
Resting there, so unevenly

I almost want to reach down
And adjust myself.

The peevish store salesperson
Wants to know what I

Think, blinking enthusiasm
Into blue florescent

Lights, but I can't
Loft any shots into

Its pregnant net. I long to
And on the way, feel

The ball, riding dribble up my side,
Clinging close like a friend, and

The three of us: basket, ball
And I will remember the last

Time we met in other forms,
In another life — where a kind of

Genetic faint memory
Allows me to re-enter

The honeysuckle,
Where I will breathe

Hard into the chambers of
The contentious ball,

Like a heart, and regardless
Of how tall or bent or halt or

Stupidly taciturn the hoop stands
Before me, it won't matter for

I've become a player, after all.

NO BASKET IN LAS VEGAS

For Bob Broughton

A wind gusts in the net,
A breathing thing
Somewhere, as bright
As any neon and
I seek a basket in Las
Vegas, stand outside
A theatre feeling too much
Like the Great
Duse, who died on
The steps of
One, trying to
Get in. I want
A gym, though I'll settle
For a basket someone
Has thrown in
A lot or the desert
Of open parking
Space. I find maitre-d —
Who can get
Anything in a big-shot
Moment, even a basket —
But gathering up
My needs for even
A net falls short.
How about UNLV's gym
Boxed up way across
The lot, as if for
A cargo shipment
To a basketball-rich
Midwest? There's got to
Be a school.
I would be satisfied
With one shot
And could win it
All Vegas fashion,

Wandering the Strip
Where every light's
A scoreboard. I thirst for
A full court
Game, as if spectators
Would float adrift in
Gawking. Night brings
Dismay, casino
Plays eddy and whimper,
The flowing issue of fire-
Works reaching down
For their yellow
Tails, deceptive
Falling through
Themselves like a broken
Cane seat in a small-town
Chair. It is dark
And I leave,
Sounding out night's lighted
Praise to the cabbie,
The larger-than-life
Come-ons, handouts
That float up as
We drive off. I
Follow a time-
Lapse on horizon where
I imagine the sun
As balls cast in the air,
Following each other,
Hanging three at
A time before
Falling. I
Used to be a fast
Enough shooter, but
To keep all three

Suspended before
The world… The city
Now useless as a camera
Flash from miles
Away. We drill into
The sunset, as if a pick-
And-roll is about
To twist free; the electric
Lights burrow like tiny
Push-pins behind us.
I sweat this sunrise, shiny as
The soft blue Mercedes
Feel myself yield
To its power
In this beaten Yellow
Cab, moving as if to
A winning shot, nervous
The game will end
Too soon. The ball
Dances more orange, serrated,
Moving up and down
Forming lines above
The roads like furrows
On a coach's head.
I am not delirious
From the ceiling
Of drugs or booze, leaving
Las Vegas. I just want
A simple hoop and
Backboard, the size
Of a small-town sign,
A reservoir of my days,
On the portals of a garage
So I can fly above

And look way down in
A dream before
Dunking,
And see something there —
A circular
Bone in cross-section,
Its net soft and
Moving marrow —
Out here on this
Lonely road for one
Shot on a shabby, broken
Ridge of backboard that is
All this night's
About — for one more try —
So the cabby can drive me
Home a winner.

WHERE ON THE COURT WE WERE

For Paul George and William F. Rountree, Jr.

The vacant space below
The Women's Gym in Montgomery
Hall fills suddenly with
Students, shifting by us,
Tunneling down the stairs
In the Spring flags of their clothes.
Below us Doctor George
Launches his ideas on
European History.

Hear the ruthless clasp
Of Napoleon, how he never slept,
Took catnaps. I lull Joe
To sleep and drive by. Everything
Seems about getting
Even. The French divide
The calendar into three ten-day
Weeks. By now, we're closer
And Napoleon has married
A Polish woman I can't
Name. Someone
Strokes a shot, important
As the Rosetta stone.

He says the French never bathed
For months. We leave the pocket
Of shaking floor.
I spiral the ball like fast-
Growing roses on
The trellis of a hand: Versailles,
And don't feel
The need to send out ships
Or to bathe, even if we
Chance upon great
Granaries, city states, or even
Teutonic territories.

GUIDE HAND: SHOOTING BASKETBALL

Poor stranger who's
Tagged along all

These years without
So much as a celebratory

Clasp, you grab ahold
And haul the bed

The sofa, the ailing
Father up

The narrow stair-
Well only to be lost

In the doorway,
Left to watch

What's left behind
Move away without

You.

SIDE-LINE TRAP

Start with — full-court
Freedom leading you astray —
Being led to the sideline —
The collapse — the line behind
You a menace — two defenders.
Ahh, where are your teammates?
Nobody to bail you out, no way
To drive, caught in the web
Of your own making, paying
The price for not paying
Attention. Inside the terrible
Half-circle of converging players
You stand, try to duck under
The closing trap, hitting façade of
Arm. The ball's still no one else's.
Where is a pattern you've run?
Where have your teammates turned?

You have never felt so
Enormous or so alone.

ALL THIS AND DUNKING

For Porter Spangler

I see him bound into a steep
Climb, like Sputnik,

Driven to it by what
Means we could not know

In 1958, the first dunker
In our high school. Maybe

First in the civilized world
Around us, as our team

Tried to meet him
There in the air, and failed.

But he rose, again and again.
Porter leapt like fire up

The mast as everything fell
Beside. For he had no business

Leaving the party: we
Needed him to break

Open the net like a costume hat.
By that single act of sky-

Bound earth, he had ruffled
The entire team's strings.

I rose up as if to
Discover first-hand the net's long

Blonde hair falling to waist,
And finally with the aid of Tuf-

Skin managed to rise over
The rim and urge the ball in.

When I stepped out, I was
Struck by the beautiful young

Lady who was a New York proof-
Reader, all the surrounding glass,

The sheerness of such heights.

THE STUCK BALL

The ball sulked
In the huddle of
Corner, wedged
Between the tight
Rim and backboard,

Curled, really,
Into a ball, and it
Wept. I staggered
Toward it, where gravity
In the hole, meant time
Slows, and I leapt
But failed to bring it
Down. There, watching what
Was below and all
The stars.

It withstood other
Taps, watched
What was below,
And above: the stars.
I jumped and freed
The ball with a finger-
Roll, and we
Both fell, like fruit
This jack-o-lantern
With a mind, less
An eye, this rise
On the sky, having
Fallen finally through.

DANCING BY WILT

The Stilt in silk at Sibyl's
Disco danced away the night.
He, with his date, me with mine,
And talked of a one-time roommate
Dave Fedor, who played for Warriors —
Kenny Sears and Willie Nauls, who
Joined Wilt from the Knicks.

We held court and no wild surprise
Of a dancer there dared to try and
Move us. Wilt glided, leaned over.
A bridge we all travelled under that
Carried the great names of the game:
Cousy, Russell, Robertson, Greer,
McGuire, Baylor, "Sweetwater,"
Even Gallatin, Bradley, Frazier
West, going strong after the fine
Leading lady to dance. Wilt back now
We slid the floor as at the tired end
Of some defensive drill, and Wilt
Bent down to Twist.

                    Reflecting, he had some shiny
Gold on his neck, pronounced as hornbook,
And underneath there had to be
Lessons, a page from a scorebook for
The man had scored one-hundred.
All we did that night was course
The narrow passages between the dancers —
The four of us — with the assists of those
Gone before, as celebrities swung
Away like errant doors before him, and
Lazy as a dream, the white Disco ball
Floated up the wall. Wilt pounded
With a foot that could have smashed
At any time, this gentle giant, from game
That can be found anywhere there's
Music and the same familiar dance.

THE GYM ACCORDING TO TIM BURTON

For Dennis Held

You come to a place
Where you belong,

Throw off your
Coat, like a pick,

Feel the invisible
Magic of a spider spinning

A web of net,
Bold as blonde

Locks: What keeps
You there is

The wondering notion
That no one can

Know this home
Like you. The ball lofts

Up and in, bringing
A sound so soft

That night lets day
Begin — perfect swish,

Ripped net and spider's
At it again. The basket

Squeaks, turns
A voice shadowy

And secluded. There's no barrier
And the bleachers open

Wider than a smile.

BROKEN BACKBOARD

The naked rim stands
Lid heavy, shaking

And continues to glare
Down as glass fast
Separates like overcast in

The puffs and slivers of silver-

Flowering, the dunker —
Having leapt into highlight
Reels — sits, his eyes

Frozen to the ice
Of glass that tangos
There. The game is

Stopped; the players stretch
A restless upheaval, as if
They soon will melt away.

A nearby step-ladder pinches
Open and more glass disjoins
And falls; a janitor plucks

Off the hoop like a ring
Which, for the first
Time in years comes

Free, since dunker, both
Chastised and happy, first gave it
That thundering, surrendering love.

MIAMI BEACH AUDITORIUM

All six-nine of center
Larry Foust of the Fort
Wayne Pistons charged
Off the floor and lunged

At me on the temporary
Court at Miami Beach Aud.
Where I'd run out to fetch
A kicked ball.

Scooping it in fear
I summoned all my boyhood
Strength, and as sure as next
Morning's sun in the fields

Of flamingos at Hialeah
Track, the ball surmounted
The heights of Foust
And ducked in the basket

As if summoned.
A stunned hush, momentary
As exploded past, his hands
Still high and the dome

Of his head agleam —
Sweat without a mop.
When he stepped back
Foust smiled, stooped

Enough to pick me
Up, but instead shook
Hands, wrapping
My right inside his —

Enough to transfer
Powers where the whole
World rolled to me by luck.

COURT RETURN

I had been memorized
By the beautiful court:
When I returned
The lights brightened
In adoring recognition.
And the hardwood
Fell resilient as time felt
Under my feet with the drive
It had left for me.
I worked hard all night
Not to get too excited for
The place. There was one
Opponent — those rolling hills
Before me. I looked at
The player sleeping
And between those
Hills, a draw, and drove
Around the side of another
Hill and I truly saw
For the first time in years
The hoop shining above
Like a cocoon of sun.
Though we lost that
Night I left convinced
The court protected me
When I fell, sent powers
Into my legs as I drove,
Felt the hoop lean
For me like a friend
And when the shot fell
I dropped to my knees
As if I could hug the place,
Steady in a grown man's arms.
That way you remember it.

WHAT WE DIDN'T KNOW

For GPG

Included how tablets
Of salt — just three or four
Before game-time required

Us to be watered like flowers,

And loading the iced tea
With sugar had deleterious effects.

We didn't know that Baron
Of Beef, floating big as missile in
Fat in the middle of training

Table would slow us down.

We didn't know anything
When the Server carved his
Finger and the large knife dripped

Blood all over everything, including

The roast. We laughed,
Unaware of disease.

We laughed and scratched,
And it didn't seem
To matter that the jump-

Step wasn't invented,

That we couldn't use the cross-
Over dribble — or strength
Shoes teach calves to fly.

We knew enough to
Laugh and scratch
Our way through. We won or lost,

And didn't, for a second, die.

GYM RATS IN LOVE

That pokey first
Step's intention —
Trying to stay
With him

Caught tight like
Like a middle-
Name between
Two people
About to marry...

The sweet feeding
Frenzies of
Passes, hang
Ball, for him?

He makes
Some, she stops
Eases it out,
Holds forward,

The ball in
A kind of
Ready
Surrender.

No sin —
But having
Done that,
She crosses

With strong jab
Step into
The court
Sweet spot.

He wonders why
Of all the gym-
Joints in all
The world,

She happened
To come
Into his. She calls
The game to begin.

PRACTICE

For Mark Stimpfle

The green lawn's rising toward
Scissors and the flutter of woman
Snips her grass, grasps each plume in
Hand. No wonder she is so irritated.

It must be slow at season's
End, almost the start of another
Fall what with the snow falling
In months and summer deliberative,

Ready to empty the red tulips
Of cold water, so I start shooting hoops
Here, look over, and we nod to each
Other. The rhododendron was blessed to

Live beyond transplant; the grass seed
She planted took hold in the slightest
Corner, but rubbed by the wrong-way mower
Wheel, disappeared like a newborn's

Hair. What a waste, I think, toting
Up the 600 shots I'll take this afternoon.
Neighbor eyes me. I return the look,
As if neither of us can leave this perfect

World we've planned in the hands of others.

WOMEN'S BALL

For Callie

I.
My mother, demure and shy, left
Her English classroom for mystery:
To coach the girl's team at Wellfleet
School. But her only sport was tennis,

Where films reveal her rushing
About the court in a lengthy skirt
And riding the ice of shiny platform
Leather shoes. She can't say when

Hesitant guards last stopped
At the protecting limits of half
Court, as if it held a side-line trap —
A black-line lapse above.

II.
By the time I took the court,
Girls still stopped at girdle of mid-
Point. "Drive!" but girls sized
The little gathers of their steps

Forward, buried their dribbles
Up their arms like pale offerings,
Looked for someone to save them —
Without a single man around.

III.
My daughter Callie breaks — a vagabond
Steps the aisle of half-court, is dancing
The bloom of press, blistering,
Follows rugged side-line like a guide

Into the welcome front-court as
Though she has come too far
To turn back. She rises and releases
A jumper — the ball rotating toward

Her, perfect with backspin, as if
It could turn shy at any moment
And as a man in suede next to me
Hollers out: “No way,”

Her shot curls in, burrows into
The flower pillow of net’s long
Dreams. The women on bench
Bend and straddle, pretzels in drudgery

Of every tension. The scoreboard
Marks down the time. Twenty seconds
And her shot calls money once
More, slicing half-court like a soft

Peach, and in the best way anyone
Can, she keeps on crossing the line.

GETTING THERE

I dribble, break hard for the hoop.
In the dream of scoring,
Snowy locust blossoms
Shiver through the air.

I want to get through and past
The happy smile of runway,
Curled as it is, outward,
But half a bucket. I have lived

The driveway, taken the uphill
Gallop to hoop, when net unfolds
In the mercury vapor. I have run,
Dribbled in the mud, loud

As the slaps of a lowly beaver
Tail where I would
Yo-yo the ball against the anvil
Of faceless hard ground, feeling

Ball up-thrust like a mountain
In my hand, as I watched the curious
Sky finally manage to give way to goal.
I slow for double-duty of my own

Pass, penetrate before the zone
Sets up before me. My body is recovering
From every run, following water by
Back-tracking to a secret source.

I dribble, covering the world
Complete, like droplets —
Such a fine rain of hand!

BACK DOOR

In the chide-sound of pivoting
An alliance is formed.
You will lead for having
Been over this ground first
And are passing knowledge
Through your feet like lightning,

Watch the birches dispossess
The path itself, the grateful burning

Grunts of heavy leaves smothered
That will say where you are, that
The backdoor is always open,
The defender, up-clad in certain
Knowledge you will receive the ball
Far away on the wing.

The basket forms its laundry
And in the soft breeze of swarming

You wonder if it is
Overfilled, but you feel your
Hand flash the signal to the point
Guard, humble talisman to brothers,
And turn, turn like an echo, imparting
Everything for a basket, suddenly

Thoughtful as if turning for keys, hat,
Umbrella. No eye-gaze, no backpedaling.

The basket wallows, waiting, like
A happy joke known only to you
And your teammate. The pass

Slices to you, and shaken
Like dust from your feet,

The defender trails. You're following
Old ground and the path accepts
Your steps. The closing basket offers
Shelter now, landscape
Of open, green possibility and crossed
Trails, like brother's blood.

Beyond the narrow beak of false lead.
Neither sneak nor thief, you arrive home
At a welcoming basket
With a white wave, streaming colors,
Where you enter, smile, as though you
Finally understand your family,
And they, for the first time, you.

TREES OF YOUTH

You hunker down in the post for this is
Your place handed over by the family
Of your team. Tradition. You are like starts
Like weeds that make yourself known
But you are tall in this all-too early
Grade. You are the strange, awkward wood
Of yourself knees leaving hardly anything
Like accusation to lean upon. You step back
And send your opponent down without
A blow and soon you await amid the garden's
Fast awakenings. You will attack. But now before
Somewhere on the loosely cast forest floor
The small animals sway into jab steps
Rise up onto their filling shoes. The opposition
Post player sinks lower and lower bangs against
All. The forest is gathering now as long and wide
As the city of a shrill game-plan. The small animals have
Not left and suddenly the floor begins to move.

TEAM PHOTO

I face down the hoop
And with every lame attempt
Must look in the mirror

Of the glass board clinging
To the silver of my hands,
So the world comes back

To me, the chin of rim held
High, until the camera iris lies
Open long enough to focus

And a team resurfaces from paper
Like old headlines, raising
Hopes that someday we'll rise

Beyond the pose, into a dresser
Drawer to restore the image

That we can climb
Beyond the hidden ladder.

UNIFORM DAYS

Uniform days when silk puckered
at the waist and the elastic took up
the slow slack the letters' excess edges dripping
from the thread like webs. The numbers looked
out no longer sit alone a patch to fill empty
longing. All parts of my body climb into
the uniform at once having taken leave of other
seasons. I fight to see the block of numbers
lined up on lockers waiting to be called
team as if the colors the patched-up waists
the shoulder straps thin and already rolling up
around hangers could speak. I ford the blue
waters Wellfleet trunks shrunken from first
wash climb the high wall with my leg
as I hold the fire and ash that belong to Winter
Park ride into the soft bloom of garnet and gold
a sunset peering to the frame of a window
you emerge in wanting to be called out by number
in love or hate hear the fire of your son's hot shooting
hand lapping like a rich red fabric in the breeze
called out in the nourishment of cloth.

AUBURN GAME

Where the Boys Are stayed
Long enough to watch

The night before and we thought
We recognized Castille

From last year's team, a looming
Behemoth in one crowd

Scene, and we cheered him
Endlessly across the street,

But clearly Frank
Gorshan underwater drew

The most laughs. We signed
Autographs, my first,

For a few bored kids
Who might still remember.

Dave's hook, stopped from
A full-speed run at the foul

Line where he spun an
Arcing one-hander at the neutral

Site of Columbus, Georgia,
Flat pastures of white hair

Of coaches Kennedy and Eaves,
Symbolic of all that

Experience and feeling
The sense of uneasiness

When running the pattern
That opposition-coach

Invented — a hard-cut
I made into a forest

Where I thought I'd
Never return.

PLAYING WITH STARS

Whose reflection glances
At you with the fire of spot-

Lights you will recognize

On the freeway of the fast
Break, where they
Find you ducking in
Alone.

They are a fire
That moves in
Low, leaves high,

Into the terrible arms of
Scarecrows.

On their jumps the floor
Falls away, and you
Are left hanging,

A solitary bulb
Flickering like static
That will flare

In the sweeping wind.

"FOUR HACKING INDIANS" (Hoopfest, 2008)

For Lux Devereaux

Four Hacking Indians will pull
  No punches, as the words would
Have it, when it comes to
  Takeaways. Nothing is worse
Than driving hard for the basket
  And realizing that, when you're
There, the ball's behind you.
  I think of Lux who, I learn,
Is a team member, summon
  Memory of long net at Spokane
Falls, when we played. A dust cloud
  Of gray now circles his head,
As with mine. Have his hands
  Slowed? I think of the heavy hitters

Watching strong-armed players
  Outside O'Doherty's Irish
Grill, struggling to hold up
  Slaps — I never knew Lux
To play unfair. I remember I clamped
  Him hard on defense, saw no
Windfall of ball from me, as he
  Scored and scored. I might
Call someone I know who is now
  Living just outside Reservation
And ask for advice. Lux needed little
  Delicious space to get off a shot. He'd
Sometimes head-fake, duck under, pull
  Up and let go of the mid-range
Jumper. In close, he played above himself.

Any serious slaps were warm-hearted
  Placed on the opposition for good
Play. Where's the levity left in
  The game? The Four Hacking Indians
Must have it. Still, we must get back
  To fundamentals: Don't bring the ball

Down, anyway; you must play above
  Your head; remember how
The referee can declare your hand
  A part of the ball. Lose the ball
And you can expect to glance hard
  At your hands, as if they hang
There in blame. You're bound to
  Look up, surprised, when the air's
Heavy with loose balls balls, which
  Rise fast as morning mist in the
Pasture, seeing the ball dampen, having
  Grown eerily dark and heavy as sleep.

Doubtless, any opposition would not
  Consider it worth worry, would they
If in team selection, they drew
  "Kenneth Lay's IQ"? There's absolutely nothing
Else that my scouting report can say
  About the formidable Four Hacking Indians,
Except they don't really hack too much. Their
  Hands are too quick and accurate for that.

STAND-UP JUMP SHOOTING

For James Stephens III

Let us stand
Up, rising

Out of nowhere

Special as
Crocuses, fluted

Becoming like hoops.

Everywhere and no
Where, wait

Like a tiger, or if

The uniform is
Calm,

Be the traveler

In the swale
Of passing light

And when the small

Train, that's "point"
Contours the court

Inside, and casts
The ball out, surprising

As a first present,

Be disinterested;
The child whose

Scribbles fill a circle,

Once-open as hoop.
Knowing you can

Break the thick net,

Spaces of game
Open, you stay there,

As if you can't

Move off a strong
Pivot foot.

Keep on finding

The next comfortable
Locale, and finally be

Where the common-

Place will matter,
As you stroke

The deciding shot

That has reached and
Come to you.

SHOT ARM

The game shot arm
Has taken on too many throws
Fails with falling birds
That tremble at the end In the iron

Death of locker rooms the texture
Of pain rises You feel in the sinew
Of lame muscles the pain ridging

Atop the tired flex your power-
Sling has that night and many before
Propelled ball & now tightens Strings
Pull on the underside through the whole
Arm that has carried entire teams since

Childhood the head of a go-to scorer
In front feeling the power abuse You do
Any pain past feel blame offering
Release above valve as if it amends
At your rend of that shot you almost
Pulled through air but didn't the way
Gloom passes light through avenue of
Train even plane as you rest there
Changed like light on the farm where
You were not born but raised on this night

You ride to speeded up destinations
Turn with pain that runs into
Itself a cockpit auto-pilot
Surrounded with conditions
The buried isolate where the wet
Compass places everything Blame
This unpatched nuance your shooting
Arm feels on the turn any arm
Feels as you return your shot
To the land of baskets Four nights

Straight of shots   that were   not dreams
But the palming off   of a single
Fade-away the defender within
The equal   disarray of arm the release
Looking at the merciful put-up the bight
In the wordless silence   shot takes out
Of air and ankle   helping unto sinking
Ground the peppery landing   There is
So much to remember   so much
Forgotten in wall of everything   slung
Like game photos   after losing defenders
Jumping   too soon   on the run-out where

You go without them   go up   wanting only to be
Overcome with joy   knowing for once
Before the thrust   levers   the go-around
Where everything shines   like a Band-aide
And you can't   say why   you did it You fell
On the break a surface bruise that will not
Heal a scar of defeat the location you point
To as if it's also   nothing smothered in the blind
Answer of another's greater wound by now
Feeling throbs like a drum you   didn't
Follow ancestors   at Pea Ridge where
The horse has just   gotten its head and whirls
Against you a picket fence   no irate coach
Ever delivered numbness of poor Antietam
The temperature   strict as winter
On a Greyhound   bus you've reached at last

The gloom the gauzy sky soreness till
There   days months later   but you
Wish it broken more quiet is   this nightfall
Than ache you've taken   with the ten-thousand
Shots   and so the pressure builds   for more

For all to go in like screws on a press
Bed   the metal you cut in the intaglio
Of your life which is now   buried buckshot
Emerging from the wood   the bones squeaking
Like a spruce ladder after four coats have been
Removed   the branch of arm as you res t
The head of   your ball   in your hands having
Lost the will to life itself

Against your own
Wasted moment   it was the last wonder
The home crowd   that too belonged where
Dreams lay in fragments   as it passes   this train
Beside   and over and above and a passenger plane
Casting new shadow   over the spirit of the farmhouse
And red- tunnel barns as you look up   at the shot   listen
To the silence of   one night one victory overtaking you
With the rumble of engines   feel the surprise
Of sensation's   blur of every arm   you have
And like the phantom   the pain   of the wound that
Is and isn't   there   is the return of   the shooter's
Touch that flew You feel it kicking in something
That never will leave   the moving thing's
Return   alone at season's end   the glorious lost part.

THE RULE OF VERTICALITY

In a room above
You alone reside —

A private place with a chandelier
Of shining net.

Your arms straight as walls,
As if to keep out intruders,

Hear the whisper of climbed
Stairs, find someone

Has risen above you.
You freeze

As the place is full of
Lifting arms and falling,

The sky above has come
Down with fast clouds.

You spill in delicious descent
Your invited soul.

PLAYING WITH CONTACTS

The pool of action's eclipsed
As I have dropped

To my knees, afraid
To come back up without

Expensive plastic.
It's as though sweat

Has come out with its
Own eyes to watch —

Every eye is watery
There as we search and fail

The long minutes to find
The world of this globe,

Big as a tear that will
Reflect congealed light.

My teammates tip-toe
Like faulty dancers

Across the rolling shadows
Of themselves, dropped

Like eggs.

        I have no history
Of finding them, save

For the night at Howden's
House where a lens stood out

Like a lost Halloween
Eye, pool drained.

On my upturned
Finger a small bead

Appears, sweat dripping from
Within, and I will be

Restored, my eye
Will decide everything

As I see the hoop fall
Together, and become,

In sharp focus,
A needless beacon.

HOME-COURT ADVANTAGE

A shot rustles through
The trees as I heave

My body's abandon
Out from behind the bow

Of a corroded kerosene
Barrel. Your shot rises

From a pebbly gravel
But you maintain your

Footing. I am thrown
Into a stunted jumper

From beneath the slivered
Paws of pine. The ball

Splashes, circles and drops
Like a lazy child.

What is already there in
The will that shapes all falling?

I harbor the distance
To the basket, the secret inlet —

This hour spent shifting
My weight, swinging forward

Lunging out — a bear protecting
Its eternity of cave, beneath

Wood. I use terrain
For my trick shot

And bulldoze away —
Under, over, through like

Water, leave this home
Court, go out into the world

Where I don't know which
Pebbles loosen, where

Springs emerge in rivulet
Where all the heart's

Court hides relentlessly
Waiting to be discovered

Like a familiar face
So close to home.

SPINNING ON FINGERTIPS

For John Broughton

An internationalist might see the globe
Controlled by one person
Or government; a western historian
Might only hear stand-off in a desert
Town, the slap of leather as everyone
Draws. To the mother of a player
The spin might suggest the force a ball
Holds over child, the dreamer chasing
To regain the dream of control in air;
A hard-working parent might envision
The need to work hard to stay in
Place; the coach might see this as pure
Fancy to impress; the player a way
To pass time before the buzzer
Drills like cicadas in the air; an aesthete
The moon suspended in dizzying
Haze. To me, the ball was but ornament,
Bright as new blossoms on a fruit-laden
Orange tree. Such display must surely
Tell teams a lot about the physics
Of inertia, of how in a flimsy world
Where we find all sometimes topples
And rises and spins in its own
Perfect space in this lovely unfurling
Of form and function — this hand that
Can, believe, only open unto grace.

GAME FACE

For Kenzie

The little girl frowns
Trying on her game
Face, like make-up. Anger
Fused with sweetness.

“Don’t get mad,” someone is
Always bound to
Say. “That’s not right,”
Faster than one can

Wipe the confident
Exercise of a smile
Away. She stutter-
Steps from the tiny

Eddies of players,
Bolting from where
She seemed so
Stuck in place.

SHOOTER'S ROLL

I arch another twenty-footer
And the shot clangs, rides rim, and falls.
"Shooter's roll," a flat-top kid cracks

I don't need to show
Off with a gauche swish.
I fire again; ball and net meet like old
Lovers, lacing and unlacing.

"Shooter's roll," a boy snickers
Already acquainted with irony.
Now several players, lazy with skill,
Stand watching as I spin

A shot that rolls off stiff fingers. Now
I'm aware of what they see: my paunch,
My shirt too tight, my caved-in shoulders.
They're not awed or even resentful, just

Impatient. This is not Georgetown they've taken
Over Princeton in the office pool. They want
Me to leave. They don't have Jordon's moves,
As I watch them stroking the ball like a child

That is about to go home, and soon return to
Express its simple love. One shoots and swishes
His new-prize shot. The net climbs up, as it goes,
The way socks are pulled up when there's work to do.

DRIBBLING IN THE STREET

The ball stands high
As you test its bounce, soon

Tall before your eyes
It leads you home,
Following an eagle
Toward a distant nest,

Using all this driving
Room as you pick a faster
Pace, follow its

Bounce off the curb.
In snow. Palm the ball
At a traffic light. Wait
And release. You will

Not limit yourself to the soft
Velour of hot blacktop, sizzling
Like the hands of a torrid shooter.

Gradually, your fingers accept
The stubbornness of its return.
The ball attracts the eye of a stone
And recoils off course. Before long,

The sidewalk's hand-
Rolled, and the dribbles
Line up precisely

As if waiting to arrive
But two young girls drive
Close, honk and slow,

In charge, and you
Look down at the ball
Brimming with

Energy, and wave
As if clearing
Out for the last-

Minute drive
That will seal
The victory. Twenty,

Fifteen, ten
Seconds. Eight...
They linger

But you must burst
To the basket.
The pistons drum

Like fingers by
Your side: now
Everything's part

Of your hand —
And it is finally full.

BAD DUNK

I.
Today's players reach
Yards away from
The basket before

They fly
And flush ball
Down the chute

Like dirty laundry.
No pacing
Like a pole-

Vaulter, no need
For heaven and earth
To line up. Bless

Them for there's
No need for sky
To stretch out

And wait, to
Hold up
Its own.

II.
I am falling through
Myself, faster than
The ball, the hoop,

This experiment where
The air ebbs
Out an effort

And I climb
The best
My slow

Twitch muscles
Will permit.
I jump again,

The way a bad
Elevator will
Surprise

With a lurch
Before the top
Floor. The shot well

Placed on rim —
My stomach
Climb after my

Own heart, to
Burden the front
Lip of hoop

Only a finger
Dip. My
Dunk's more

Like reaching
Into a cookie jar,
But sensing

Everyone bemused
And watching
Like a mother,

I quickly withdraw
My hand. The steps
Fall with me, and

The ball tunnels,
Goes in blind-
Folded, a little

Faster than usual,
A shy night
Visitor. At my best,
Hands left in Tuf-

Skin, feeling tacky,
I climbed until
I lost my footing

Before I landed as
If to say what
A place I have

Seen, remembering
For all who will
Listen at Sweet Shop,

About how a ball
Eased across the rim and
As if a convergence

Of stars had lined up
Fully, the net bobbing —
Bouquet in blue moonlight.

AIRBORNE TIME-OUT: NCAA'S 2006

For John Olney

The second half emerges
Like a wild drunk as
Players on both teams

Strut, dunk, loop, climb
And land again, completing
Themselves in air, crash

Trying to save what little
They have conquered up
Till now: a three-

Point lead that will erase
Itself in the soft
Flesh of a record book.

A guard starts by flying through —
But out of bounds, wrestling
With the suspended state of ball,

Surrounding it with the choice mass
Of his right hand, and high above
A tussling swamp of photographers,

He manages the hug of hands into
A "T," trying to stay like a God on the mantle
Of air which will contain him — a half-

Second fusion, where this time
The referee follows close, his head
Down against the sideline like a rescue

Dog, sees him free and floating
There, and lets him down easy.
The photographers captured his

Display, but on the late news, no
Manufactured freeze-frame can possibly extend
The moment better, render the secret powers

Speckled like ions, where a skilled
Athlete gets a chance to win over
The twin battles of time and gravity

And have time to remember how glorious
It felt while rising, never to fall.

ALFRED'S TOSS

For Mark Palek

Defensive stop before
Half-court, Alfred

Pulled up the cliff
Of his high dribble,

Held the ball
Like his frightened

Face, and let it fly
Straight up in space.

Fans groaned and
Said, "The basket's

There," not on
The ceiling or behind

The chair. Time softens
Foibles after all

The years: errant
Plays we talk

And fear. I decided
Long ago, shots

Fall in the forest
Uncertain as

Snow. They go
Or don't

One cannot
Know, who will

Hear them and
If they fall;

From just a heave,
Or well-aimed

Ball. Alfred's
Toss came at

No cost, he
Neither won,

Nor lost.
From that deep

Spot, he let it
Fly, for everyone

Must get one shot.

TRASH TALK

"The players should yell, fake, harass, worry, annoy, and bully the opposition into such a state of frustration that they will be willing to give up the ball just so the turmoil will be ended."

Coach Garland F. Pinholster
From *Coach's Guide to Modern Basketball*, 1953

We know no argument's ever
Done. Gathering the rhythms of
Your movement, I still take
The fake and follow it helpless
Into the air — this parting where
You go your way and I, mine.
From silent code of a head bob, swing
Of a ball fake ripping like a circular

Saw, I step back and see
You draw on the hoop, strike
As you drive into the branching
Arms, the forest one strives to become

But cannot, and then you turn
Vulgar, say enough to me on top
Of the score that all the baby
Carriages turn over and trash
Plugs sewers in a ten-
Block area, I decline to stand
Up to you, already draped word-
Ready, Garland, Coach, you never
Meant to turn a brush into curse —
Make language of game no longer of
Baskets made, strategy or hustle-play
Or the peeling pursuit of ball across
The floor, but of coarse language.

And should, by some fate, the ball lodge
Against the rim, like a word in
The throat, sit endlessly beyond the lazy
Leaps, looking more like a circle of
Words above your cartoon head, I'll
Wait patiently to see how long
It takes to return to game, bury
The near-forgotten point in
The deft, voice-softening net.

PICKING TEAMS AT FIFTY

For Dr. Don Schmitt

Haul myself
To center

Court and smile
To see players

Who recognize
Each other —

Familiar as twins
In self-same

Clothes, uniform
Shorts baggy

As the blurring
Rupture inside

My over-grown
Stomach. This

Hurts to sink
To this level

And find myself
Treated lower

Still, where
Senior dis-

Counts don't
Help — hoping,

Hopeless. I join
The center to round

Out my exercise,
Club-style. Several

Selected first,
Saunter together,

Take property
Of the left

Basket, as peripheral
Vision of grey

And white hair show
Up, popping off

The screen like
Something out of

Black & white
Movies. A reluctant

Wave takes me
Across to a place

Outside on wing,
Selfless as a helping

Verb, always the last
Picked. Still I

Am comfortable,
But the game turns

Its back on me

A player now
And then tossing me

A look as if I can-
Not be trusted but

The legs under
Me can still

Carry the full
Length of the short

Court. I go up
Onto my toes,

Ready to climb
Into a stand-

Up jumper, but
I never got fed

As if time
Doesn't matter

To the young.
When the point

Hand-delivers it,
And takes it back,

As if I'd never
Had the ball

For my own...
We lose; I don't

Score. I sit on
The cushioned side-

Line court chair
And the moment

I do, dust rises.

DEATH OF A PLAYER

For Gary Schull

When the last of Wake
Forest's players appeared

As we stood on the court
At the all-year reunion

He last turned
For a photo, his hair

Graying slightly, smiling
The same generous smile,

The mascot standing in yellow
Stripes like slats of sunlight...

The picture shows
7:47 left till the half-

Time ends. He built
Houses, he said,

And his massive heart
Died massively.

Still, I see him post
Up, stretch a body out,

Shoulders spread like
Wings, taking up a greater

Place in the lane
That no one can

Ever fill again.

TOO LONG IN THE LANE

The jab step yawns
Like a lazy hound dog.

Loneliness stands with me
In the lane, hinterland
Where even the thin will
Be forced to become
A post — a bulwark
Against the tentative tide

And rush of flesh, last bastion
Of something you once did, and did
Well. If you are short, you don't
Ever belong inside, and even
If you're tall you get three

Seconds' worth, forced to make
Your point — a short
Speech in a long
Debate to clear

Everybody out, make your shot,
Establish who you are. You must be
Teaching kindergarten — kids
Dragging down your arms.
Most of the playground

Balls need inflating.
If you are my age and have
Played high, even backed in
Against Bill Cowens — if only in
Jest — someone's said you're

Too long in the lane and you
Probably are. After all,

The entire court stretches annually
And will take everything —

Longer strides, greater
Range of motion, suffering for
The broken wrist — a blood-
Feeding bone that rocks
Your hand with each shot,

But once you hear
The traction-skid
Of a scalloped Nike you'll
Slip into your rags —
Twelve-year-old Converse All-Stars —

Pop out where you can
Range like a horse, take
Someone, anyone, to the hole
Like a blind suitor

Or launch one from God's
Country, the shot from the guts
Of the universe there
Atop the key, as if the crown

It made above the foul line
Was placed there for your head alone.

You rise up in a rebellion of flesh
With only
A body heavier
By the years left to tilt
And swing below
The ball's infectious flight.

THE WHITEST SNOW

The night is a row of sunset
Banked with snow, but no

One sits on the seats
Below. I arch the ball over

The corner limb. It brushes
And bursts a dusting on

The crown of woe — my head
Frozen blue, my hands

Red and heavy. Then net
Struck blind with ice

Looks out unseeing
As I unhand the ball

From my stiff grasp.
Free to wander the frigid

Hill at home,
Each shot a small

Stomp and then a jump —
I know where I am,

Twenty-two feet from
The hoop watching myself

In the ball's upward
Climb, over the wire lines

To the basket and find
The whitest snow, where

No one has sullied with
Steps but me, where

The winds settle into drifts,
In the bodice-thicket of snow

Where I am thrown
Into helplessness of distances.

My elbows restore their bend
Into the perfect emptiness

Of the repeating sky.
One long snowy shot, after all

This, where I must not
Grow cold, or admit it, and

Continue to navigate
As if I had ordered

The weather to stop
Everything in the brush-

Strokes of snowy shot,
With no particular

Season.

LETTER TO SAM JONES

For Terry Trueman

As we descend from basket down to foul
Line, the ball is scattering a loose crowd
Of oak leaves for me to rake later.
As many years as leaves, here I am
And I wonder where you are. I don't know
If you'd remember that I beat you on
That summer day side-court where
Home court combed almost every
Shot we fired — with more scrapes than
I had in the entire game of youth.

I'm sorry it took the judgment of a vanity
License plate that read "Celtics" for me to
Recognize you, sitting upright as a model,
Everyday citizen in that wood-paneled station
Wagon. I have forgotten the year, forgotten
The score, exactly, but I think I remember the last
Shot running down the nylon.

I remember the scar
Of the landscape: the kerosene barrel that
Dripped and smelled a footstep-path away
Toward the creaking hinge of Tom's Bowl
Shop, I remember the wind of my shot
Building in my breath and the ball slumping

In my hands one last time before I would
Seal the game. I hope I lost to repay you
For your kindness: The pat of encouragement on
The head at game's end, the magnanimity
Where I thought you Bill Russell.

I wondered if you really tried. Even a little bit.
And did nature, the great shot-blocker intervene?
Did the oak tree stand in the way of bank
Shot? Or were you just lolling along,

As you hid, looked out from behind things,
Like a fugitive? You peered up at the telephone
Pole, that dark, giant toothpick that spread
The teeth of broken concrete, and to the slab
Of unforgiving backboard, which confirmed
What you no doubt already knew: the world's
Really a stacked deck, but still we get up and play
Our foolish hearts out for someone with a towhead
And a bully friend whose arms are big as a tree.

A HOOP FOR YOU

For my grandchildren and their grandchildren, and on…

When you see my arms circled
Like a hoop, see me standing
Ready to take a shot, like a boxer's
Face, like Jack Broughton,
Considered "the father of modern
Boxing," I'll accept the backboard
Tosses like a grown-up, the ones
That more than glance,
Strike me mostly in the nose
Or groin. Know that I'll stand
And take it like a relative should.
Hear me creak in the floor
Boards, I've loved this game
Like a fresh new morning's life.

Once I've been forced to put
Away the Converse and fight
To hold my blood pressure,
As I feel it course my
Body, run its long and tired
Lines, I'll still be out there
For you, bowing my arms
Making the hoop shift in the air
To catch the ball. There's an outside
Chance you inherited a bit
Of a shooter's touch.

MIDWEST PORTRAIT

The old men gather at the pedestal
Of day to kibitz through

Coffee, amid the clatter
Of plates, insistent as rims,

Sometimes stepping out
Of the crossed certainty

Of small gyms to State,

Where the distance
Behind the ballast of glass

Backboards magnifies time, this
Easement leading to a distant

Wall where one hovers.
It is before or after the game.

The boy stands

Holding the ball at his
Side — a friend in a hammer

Lock; the boy's frightened,
Though he will appear

Safe living in the sent corner
Of the barn, where the basket

Holds court, drapes over
The dark and muddy net itself —

Like a natural defense of animals.
The ball ramps

Into his hands and he turns,
Pours the plenty of a one-

Hander, scoring once again
Against himself. A tractor

Clashes with the transitory
Nearby earth. He appears so

Tired — unaware of where
He is, that he will be remembered

Here for a hundred years.

FAR-AWAY GAMES

For Connie

After waiting I rise
Like a crane to see one
I know on the tarmac

And wonder why my wife's
Elsewhere, unable to locate
Me: Surely she is out

Looking, can pick my saunter
From the spill of a shopping
Center for she knows me as tall,

Her father just five-ten. She
Looks shocked to see me appear
Flanked by the solidarity

Of six victorious Boise State
Players who stand like spires, waiting
The harvest of luggage game balls.

Voices deepen as she gets closer.
With squirrel hunter's eyes
They survey her, old enough

To be their mother, or lover.
Luggage bolts down-chute to us.
I see the light on her face. She smiles

But looks up, as if realizing after
All these years I'm short, growing
Shorter still and I seem a child as she

Comes to claim me, kisses me
And we embrace for all to see.
I come to myself

Taller, a child, husband, father,
Teammate from a distant court.

THE DEAD SPOT

Who's that tromping
On the hardwood as if
Breaking kindling, this
Unfeeling thing of
Knocking unto no
Answer, searching
An hour before game-
Time for the dead thud
To rise like an unsteady
Dribble past the ball?

The ball sounds
Down but becomes
Buried in the buzz of
Fluorescents You dribble on
Leading with a head
Turned to work the quick-
Sand where the faulty ball
Must descend in some
Critical moment so
Low the animals awaken
In the unfolding of caves.

You know you must
Find it, lift this unfeeling thug
Off the floor so you strike and
Strike with some effect.
And failing even to invoke
This smallest ring of silence —
This knot below
Darkness that cannot soften or
Be made whole, and cannot
Lift anything, you in the above
World go on rising until
The floor gives way to
The insufferable winter night
Of fall, the echo of knowing
What's gone below.

THE FUNDAMENTALS

He'd never lost
On this home court,
The father told the stranger
As child stood watching
His father surrender
To the early Fall

Hail of corner jumpers:
Just a childhood
Game of horse until
Now. You never know
Where you'll pick up
Such a lesson — the child

Adoring his father,
His every shot. The mishmash
Of garage sale items
That stopped the stranger
Cold, first, sat like uniforms
After a game, the child's discarded

Toys spread out, the world
He knew going too fast.

LAKEN'S HOOP

Laken washed her hands of basketball
Yesterday, poised over
Her children's plastic hoop
With the tally and happy bell.
Amazed, I watched her scour dishes
In that bottomless bowl of basket.

After all she is two and now towers
Over the baby hoop, so perhaps
She found it no longer a challenge to put
Down too easily, persistent
Like her mother the cellist.

She has, in the hoop of her heart,
Made a choice to drop
The sport, to avoid throwing in with family
Tradition. One day she will turn
Pilot, and if and when she overshoots
A runway in Sitka, she'll correct, circle back
And land — bouncing like a ball
Perfect on course, at last, and there will
Be plenty of us there to urge her
On, and we'll say it wasn't

Life or death, but the slightest
Correction to the flight schedule and she
Will be safe once more below,
Tucked into low clouds.

THE WORN NET

Lies, a circle
Of string hanging
Off to one side. When

A shot arrives in line-
Drive the net jumps and snaps
Like a lariat that stings

As it destroys all
Traces of the shaggy sky.
From then on the wind

Shifts magically,
And every close shot

Pretends to go in
Following the lost.

THE FINAL SHOT

Listen while the basket
Swings away for the night
As the balls still and fall.

The regular clock drags its arms
Slow enough to cast shadow.

If it's so important why
Make it easy on myself, toss
The ball up like a throwaway?

I stand blind, having worn
Out my warm welcome for
One more chance to score
Waiting to see my shot ring
In the galloping dendrites

Of the net. I could
Die and wake up alone,
Having missed my last shot
On earth. I miss.

And broken like a net,

I remember to lock my shooting
Elbow close, release the single

Shot to send me
Home, a score to last
The rest of my life.

About the Author

Born in Orlando, Florida, Irv Broughton spent his earliest years in South Wellfleet, on Cape Cod. He started on his high school varsity as a seventh grader, and played six years of high school basketball there and at Apopka and Winter Park High Schools in Florida. After that, he had his "briefer stint" playing for Florida State University, and has continued to play what he calls "the lifetime sport" for more than 35 years.

After earning his BA and MA degrees at Florida State, Irv received an MA from Hollins College (University) in 1971. There he received an Academy of American Poets recognition. He has taught English and Communications at several colleges and universities, including Virginia Western, the University of Washington and Spokane Falls Community College. Broughton's poetry has appeared in numerous magazines including *Cimarron Review, Roanoke Review, Hollins Critic, The Iconoclast, Intro* and *Alembic.* Author of a dozen books, he is also founder of a literary magazine, *The Mill Mountain Review.*

In addition to being a die-hard, inveterate, lifetime basketball player, Broughton is also an award-winning filmmaker. Irv says he likes to carry a loose ball in his car's trunk because "it sounds as though there's always a game in progress."

Irv has three children: McKenzie, Sayer and Callie and resides in Spokane, Washington.

Terms

Finger-roll. Easing the ball off the fingers for a close-in shot, usually a lay-up. The ball literally rolls off the fingers.

Jab step. When a stationary offensive player jabs a foot forward toward the defender. If the defender backs off, the offensive player likely gains space to get off a shot. If the offensive player jabs and pulls the foot back, the defender can be drawn closer, which often opens up the possibility of an easier drive toward the basket.

Post. An offensive strategy or position where a player, usually a center or a forward, plays back to the basket — as in high or low post positions. A major offensive scheme may derive from post play. To "post up" means to establish a post position.

Rule of Verticality. Imagine the defensive player is standing completely straight up, having established position in front of the offensive player, in time. If the defender does not move, he/she is entitled to the space above the head. That's the case, even if the defender holds arms straight up.

Stutter step. When an offensive player slows or stops and shuffles feet, while maintaining the dribble. It often allows the offensive player to confuse the defender and dribble past.